D0817181

PETER PAUL RUBENS

Great Animal Drawings and Prints

Edited by
Carol Belanger Grafton

Dover Publications, Inc.
Mineola, New York

Copyright

Copyright © 2006 by Dover Publications, Inc.
All rights reserved.

Bibliographical Note

Great Animal Drawings and Prints is a new work, first published by Dover Publications, Inc., in 2006.

DOVER *Pictorial Archive* SERIES

This book belongs to the Dover Pictorial Archive Series. You may use the designs and illustrations for graphics and crafts applications, free and without special permission, provided that you include no more than four in the same publication or project. (For permission for additional use, please write to Permissions Department, Dover Publications, Inc., 31 East 2nd Street, Mineola, N.Y. 11501.)

However, republication or reproduction of any illustration by any other graphic service, whether it be in a book or in any other design resource, is strictly prohibited.

International Standard Book Number: 0-486-44830-4

Manufactured in the United States of America
Dover Publications, Inc., 31 East 2nd Street, Mineola, N.Y. 11501

LIST OF PLATES

COLOR SECTION

Plate 1. JOST AMMAN

Plate 2. JOST AMMAN

Plate 3. ANDREA DEL SARTO

Plate 4. FRANCIS BARLOW

Plate 5. FRA BARTOLOMMEO

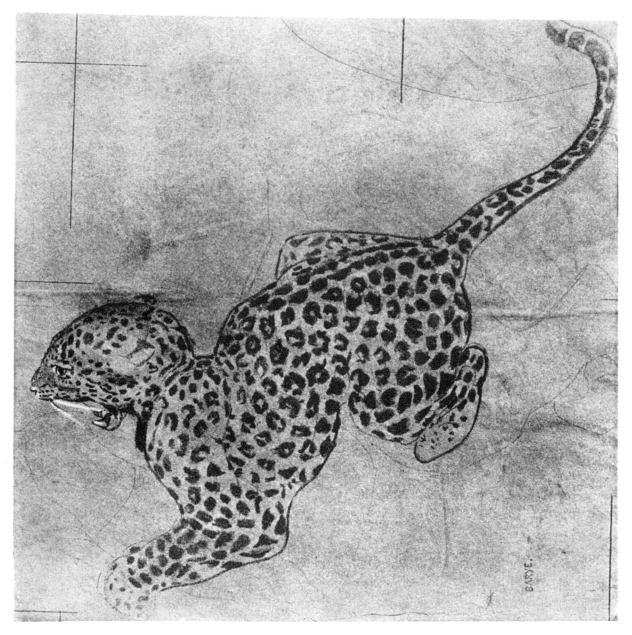

Plate 6. ANTOINE-LOUIS BARYE

Plate 7. STEFANO DELLA BELLA

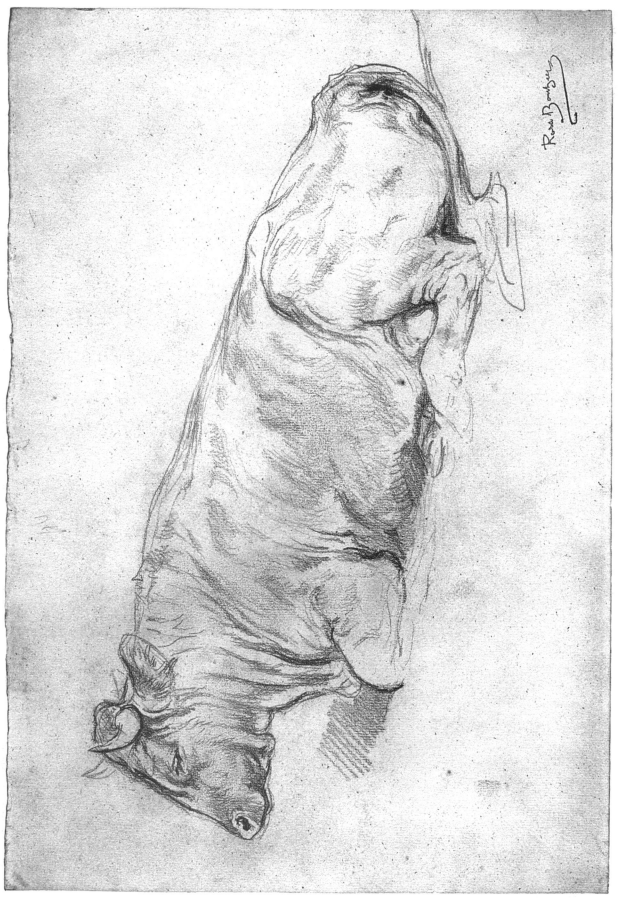

Plate 8. ROSA BONHEUR

Plate 9. HIERONYMUS BOSCH

Plate 10. EDMÉ BOUCHARDON

Plate 11. FRANÇOIS BOUCHER

Plate 12. Pieter Bruegel the Elder

Plate 13. ANTONIO DEL CASTILLO

Plate 14. Théodore Chassériau

Plate 15. GIORGIO DE CHIRICO

Plate 16. ALLAERT CLAESZ

Plate 17. CLAUDE (CLAUDE LORRAIN)

Plate 18. Edgar Degas

Plate 19. EDGAR DEGAS

Plate 20. Eugène Delacroix

Plate 21. GASPARE DIZIANI

Plate 22. ALBRECHT DÜRER

Plate 23. ALBRECHT DÜRER

Plate 24. ALBRECHT DÜRER

Plate 25. ALBRECHT DÜRER

Plate 26. ANTHONY VAN DYCK

Plate 27. ANTHONY VAN DYCK

Plate 28. ANTHONY VAN DYCK

Plate 29. Jean-Louis Forain

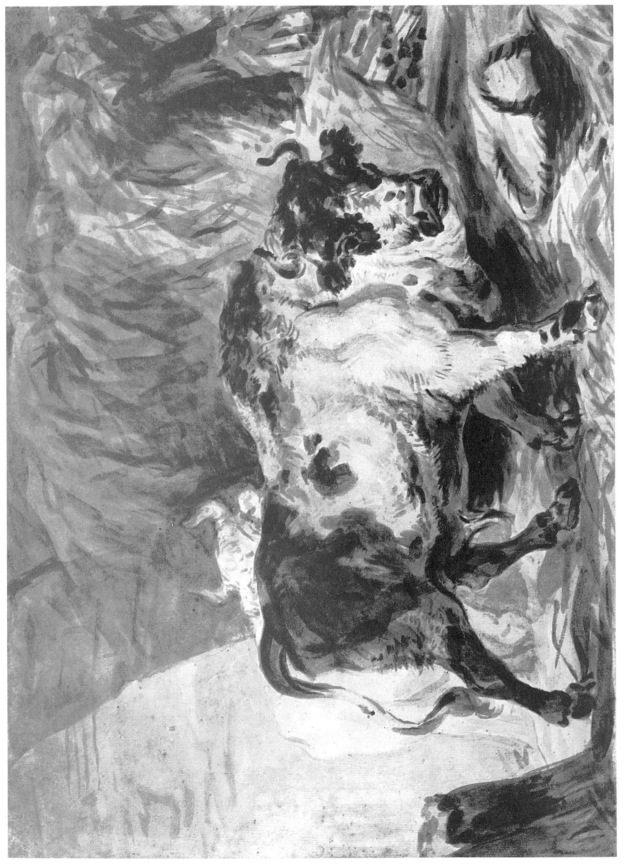

Plate 30. JEAN-HONORÉ FRAGONARD

Plate 31. Thomas Gainsborough

Plate 32. Jean-Louis-André-Théodore Géricault

Plate 33. Jean-Louis-André-Théodore Géricault

Plate 34. GERMAN MASTER, ANONYMOUS

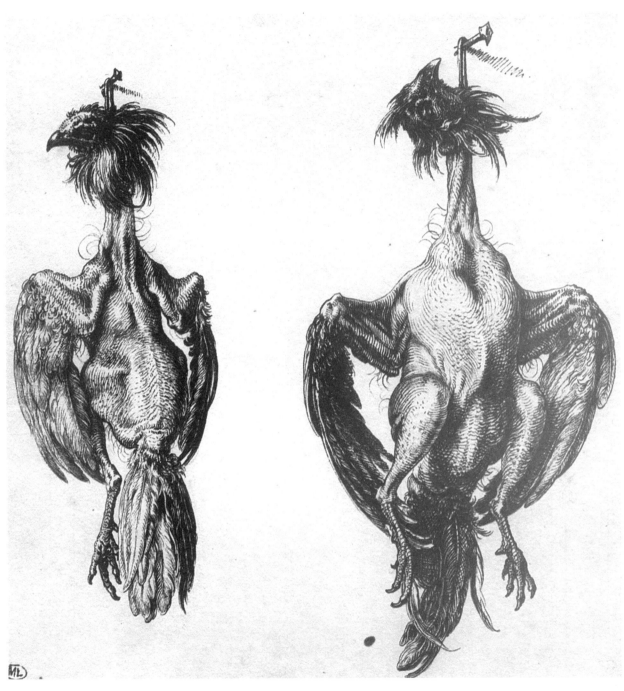

Plate 35. Jacob de Gheyn II

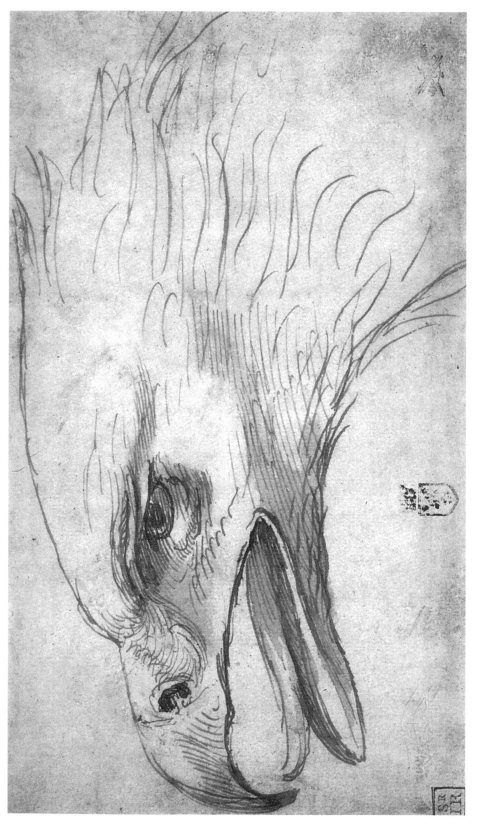

Plate 36. Giulio Pippi (called Giulio Romano)

Plate 37. VINCENT VAN GOGH

Plate 38. HENDRICK GOLTZIUS

Plate 39. Francisco Goya

Plate 40. Francisco Goya

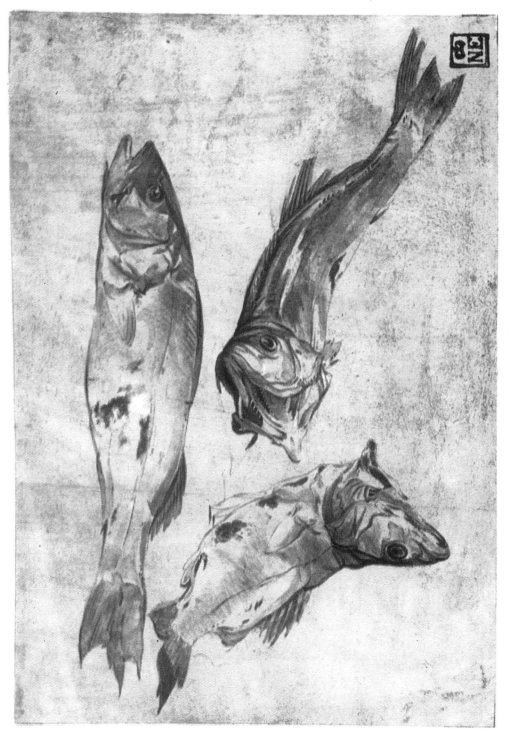

Plate 41. HANS HOFFMANN

Plate 42. HANS HOFFMANN

Plate 43. KATSUSHIKA HOKUSAI

Plate 44. Charles Le Brun

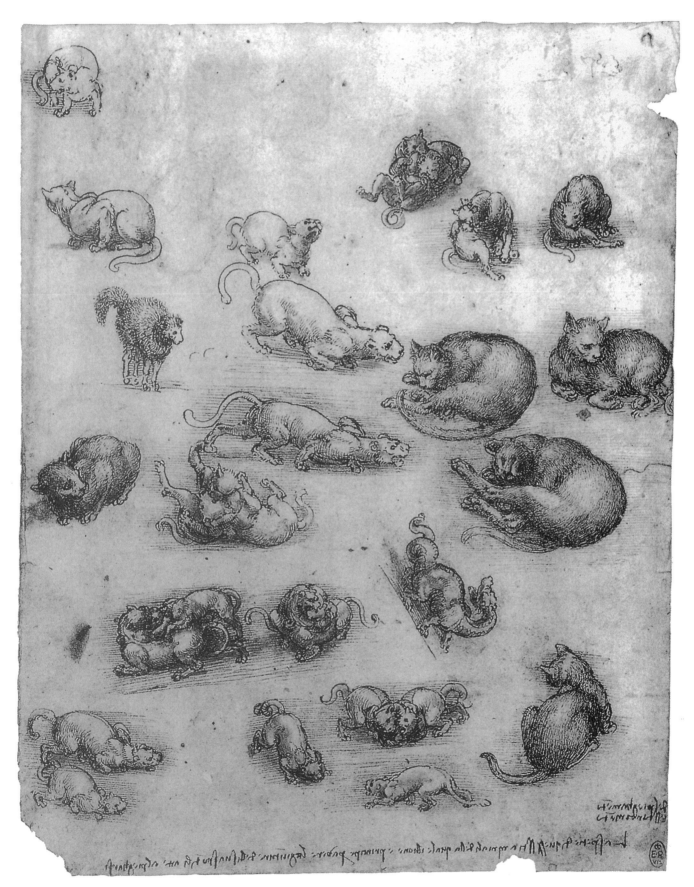

Plate 45. LEONARDO DA VINCI

Plate 46. MELCHIOR LORCH

Plate 47. HANS VON MARÉES

Plate 48. CHAO MENG-FU (WU-HSING)

Plate 49. MIDDLE EAST, MUGHAL INDIA, ANONYMOUS

Plate 50. PIERRE MIGNARD

Plate 51. Jean-François Millet

Plate 52. GUSTAVE MOREAU

Plate 53. BARTOLOMÉ ESTEBAN MURILLO

Plate 54. Jean-Baptiste Oudry

Plate 55. ANDREA DEL SARTO

Plate 56. JOHN JAMES AUDUBON

Plate 57. FEDERIGO BAROCCI

Plate 58. FRANÇOIS BOUCHER

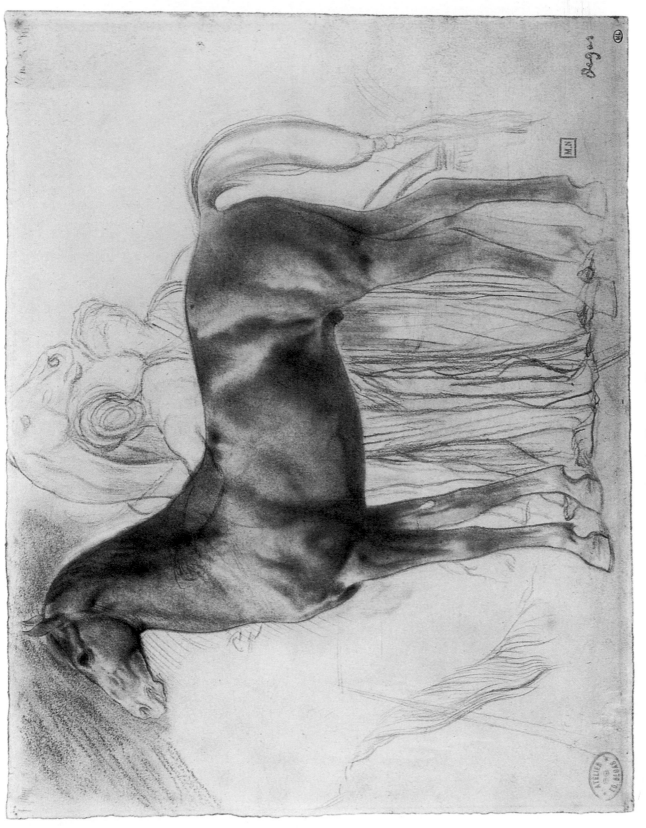

Plate 59. E<small>DGAR</small> D<small>EGAS</small>

Plate 60. Eugène Delacroix

Plate 61. FRANÇOIS DESPORTES

Plate 62. HERBERT THOMAS DICKSEE

1502

Plate 63. ALBRECHT DÜRER

Plate 64. JEAN-LOUIS-ANDRÉ-THÉODORE GÉRICAULT

Plate 65. JOHN GOULD

Plate 66. LEONARDO DA VINCI

Plate 67. LEONARDO DA VINCI

Plate 68. PETER PAUL RUBENS

Plate 69. John Macallan Swan

TROGLODYTES GORILLA mas adult.

Plate 70. Joseph Wolf

Plate 71. Jean-Baptiste Oudry

Plate 72. HERMAN PALMER

Plate 73. GEORGE PENCZ

Plate 74. PABLO PICASSO

Plate 75. PABLO PICASSO

Plate 76. PABLO PICASSO

Plate 77. PISANELLO

Plate 78. PISANELLO

Plate 79. PAULUS POTTER

Plate 80. THE PSEUDO-PACCHIA, SIENESE SCHOOL

Plate 81. RAPHAEL

Plate 82. REMBRANDT HARMENSZ VAN RIJN

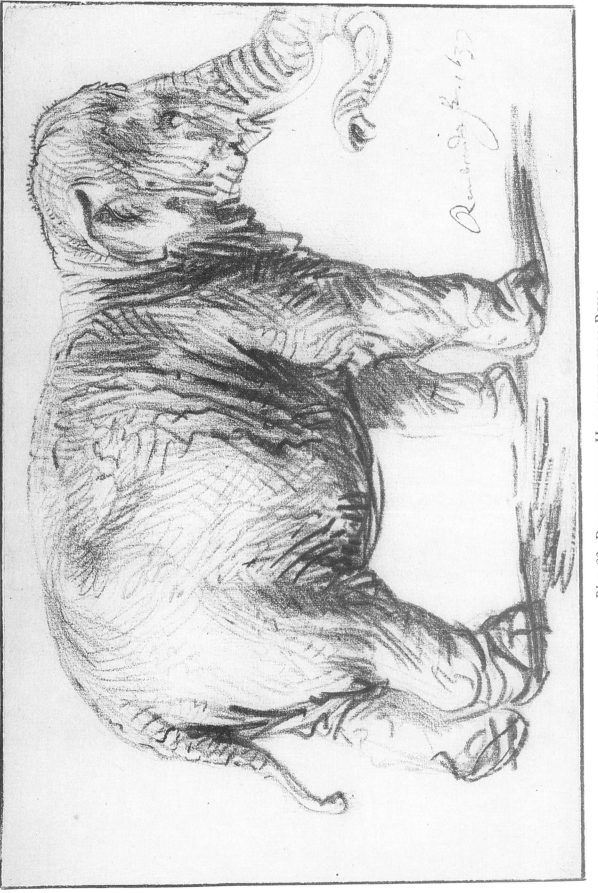

Plate 83. Rembrandt Harmensz van Rijn

Plate 84. JOHANN ELIAS RIDINGER

Plate 85. PETER PAUL RUBENS

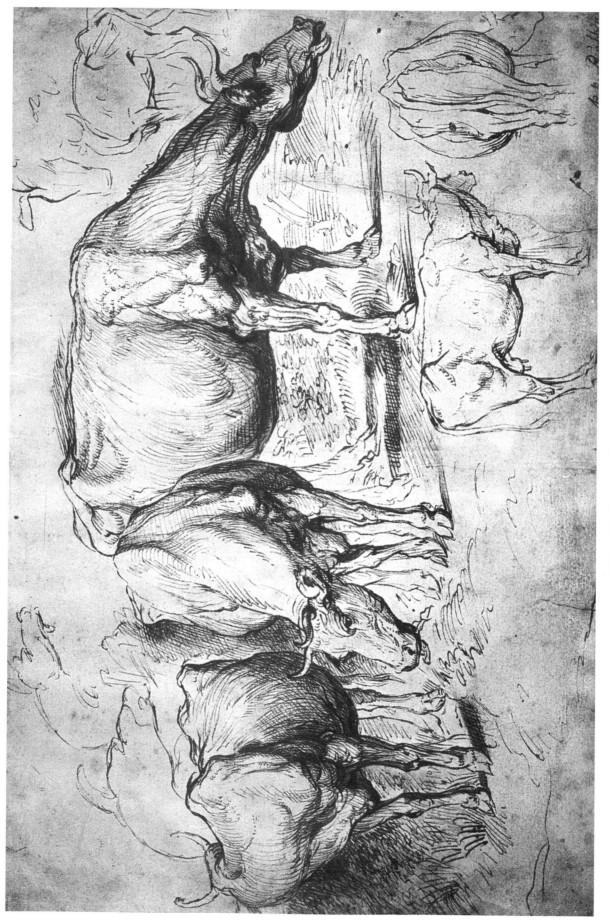

Plate 86. Peter Paul Rubens

Plate 87. ROELANDT SAVERY

Plate 88. ALFRED SISLEY

Plate 89. FRANS SNYDERS

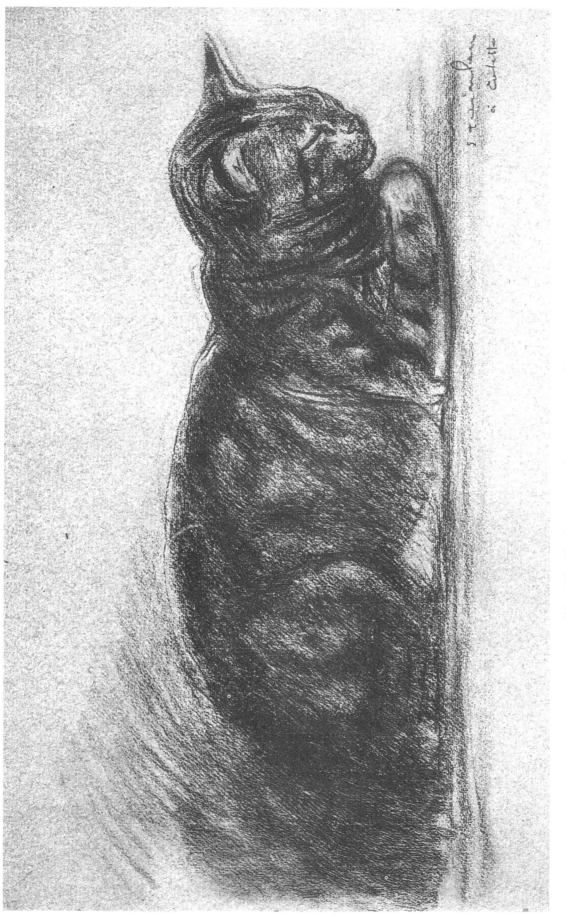

Plate 90. Théophile-Alexandre Steinlen

Plate 91. JOHANNES STRADANUS

Plate 92. Giovanni Domenico Tiepolo

Plate 93. Titian (Tiziano Vecellio)

Plate 94. TITIAN

Plate 95. Henri de Toulouse-Lautrec

Plate 96. Henri de Toulouse-Lautrec

Plate 97. Umbrian Master, Anonymous

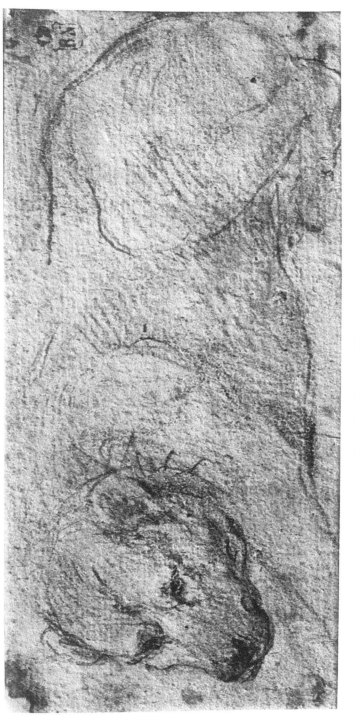

Plate 98. Diego Velázquez

Plate 99. Diego Velázquez

Plate 100. ADRIAEN VAN DE VELDE

Plate 101. VENETIAN MASTER, ANONYMOUS